Tiernan

To the Inupiat people

of Barrow, Alaska,

who share all things —J. C. G.

To Jean Craighead George,

a great friend and fellow explorer

of our great country —W. G. M.

Jean Craighead George

SCHOLASTIC INC. • New York Toronto London Auckland Sydney

Paintings by Wendell Minor

On the day Luke was born in December the wind bugled like a lost caribou calf. The temperature dropped to thirty below zero. The sun did not come up.

Luke lived in a small town beside the Arctic Ocean, not more than a polar bear's trot from the North Pole.

One day a friend, Aalak, came to visit Luke's parents.

"Your son," he said to Craig and Cyd, "needs an Eskimo name to go with his English name. That is how it is. We have two names in the Arctic, Eskimo and English."

"We have no Eskimo name to give him," said Cyd.

"You do, all right, if you want one," Aalak answered. "His name may be 'Kupaaq,' for my papa."

"We are honored," said Craig, and he smiled at his son.

Aalak picked up the baby. "Hello, Papa," he said.

That is a very different way to greet a baby, but in the Arctic, where Kupaaq was born, things are very different.

There are no trees.
The land is flat.
The sun does not set in the summer.
It does not rise in the winter.

When Kupaaq was three, Aalak showed him the winter night. The stars were enormous bonfires in the sky. Then, silently and slowly, yellow, rose, and green lights fountained up and filled the sky.

"That is *Kinuyakkii*," Aalak said. "Some call this brightness the northern lights." Aalak lifted Kupaaq high. "You and I live where the lights are born."

Aalak pointed his finger overhead. "That is our star," he said. "It is the North Star. It does not move away from us, like the other stars do. It shines right over our heads to tell the world where we are."

"It likes us," said Kupaaq.

One day in the dark of winter, Kupaaq's parents harnessed the dogs to the sled and mushed inland to the tundra lakes to fish. Kupaaq's dogs looked back to see if he was still in the sled. Seeing him, they wagged their tails.

"Gee," shouted Kupaaq. The dogs ran to the right.

"Haw," shouted Kupaaq. The dogs ran to the left.

"Hut," he said. The dogs went straight ahead.

"Look, Sisuaq," Kupaaq said to his baby brother, Sam. "I can drive. No hands."

They met Aalak at fish camp. Kupaaq helped him cut holes through the ice to the water and drop his fishnets in. In a short time they were pulling up fish by the dozens.

"Iqaluk, iqaluk," Kupaaq shouted excitedly. "Fish, fish."

When Kupaaq was tired, Aalak and Craig dug a snow cave like the shelters the old Eskimos made. Kupaaq crawled in and lay down on the caribou skins.

"Snow is cozy and warm," he said, and fell sound asleep.

When they were back in town, Aalak lowered the fish into his *sigluaq.* It was a pit dug twenty feet down into the frozen ground of permafrost. "My Eskimo refrigerator," he said proudly to Kupaaq. "Our fish will stay frozen until we are ready to eat them."

"The Arctic is very helpful," said Kupaaq.

When Kupaaq was five, hungry polar bears came to town. On Halloween night Kupaaq and his friends went trick-or-treating. His father and Aalak went out with the children, carrying their guns to warn off the bears. One came too close. Aalak shot into the air. The loud boom scared the *nanuq* back to the sea ice where he belonged.

"We did not give him a treat," said Kupaaq to his friend Uksi, whose English name was Quinn. "Will he trick us?"

"No," said Uksi. "The ocean will treat him."

"Oh, yes," said Kupaaq. "It will treat him to seal. *Yummm yummmm.*"

In the spring, Kupaaq saw millions of birds returning. The snowbirds arrived first, then clouds of ducks, and after them, miles of geese. Snowy owls flew back to the tundra and made nests on the ground.

On May the 10th the sun stayed up all night. The long Arctic day began. Kupaaq and his friends ate when they were hungry. They slept in the sunlight and they played in the sunlight.

The sea ice cracked, moved, and spread apart. Open water shone blue in the riverlike cracks. Up these leads came the whales. They breathed out spouts of mist, breathed in air, dove deep, and swam north to the Beaufort Sea.

"Good times are here," Aalak said to Kupaaq. "It is the time to go whaling."

When Kupaaq was six, Aalak took him to whale camp far out on the sea ice.

Kupaaq was greeted by Patak. "Welcome, Grandpapa," she said, and chuckled. "If you have my grandfather's name, that makes you my grandfather."

Kupaaq and Patak were given jobs to do. They melted ice to drink and helped keep the camp clean. They were told to listen to the elders to avoid danger on the moving sea ice.

Aalak harpooned a whale. The villagers came out to help him pull it up on the ice with ropes. It weighed forty-five tons.

Aalak apologized to the whale for killing it, then thanked it for giving life to the Inupiat Eskimos. He shared his gift from the sea with the villagers.

"All nature shares," Aalak said. "And we are nature."

After the hunt came *Nalukataq,* the celebration to honor the whale. It deserves a celebration. The bowhead whale is food. It is art supplies. It is fuel. Its great bones are monuments to brave Eskimos. No part of it can be sold. It is a gift to all from the sea.

At the party, Kupaaq danced Eskimo dances and sang Inupiat songs. He was tossed in the air in the blanket toss.

When he came down, Patak took his hand.

"Grandpapa," she said, "you are much too old for that dangerous game." Her eyes twinkled.

"I'm much too young," he said. "I went up so high, a bird almost ate me."

When the sun set on August the 3rd, Kupaaq slept in the darkness for the first time in three months. Summer was over. The nights grew longer and longer.

The air cooled. The sea foam froze. The blue-green ocean was freckled with ice floes. On them rode magnificent walruses going south to warmer seas.

"The *aiviQ* look very serious," said Kupaaq to Aalak.

"They are telling us winter is coming," Aalak said. "And winter is very serious."

One morning Kupaaq put on his thermal underwear, pants, wind pants, warm shirt, sweater, parka, mittens, hat, scarf, face mask, and his insulated boots. He climbed onto the school bus in the dark.

At school he took off his hat, his scarf, his insulated boots, his face mask, his mittens, parka, and wind pants.

"Alappaaq," he said to his teacher. "It is cold."

"Welcome," she answered. "Who taught you our language?"

"Aalak," he said. "I am Kupaaq."

"And I am Aalak's cousin," she said. "Kupaaq was my mother's brother. So I am your niece." She laughed at the fun of it all.

They hugged like good family members.

After school, Kupaaq, Uksi, and Patak slid down snow mountains thrown up by the big road plows. They raced in one-dog sleds. They fell off and jumped back on. They made snow caves. When they were cold they played Eskimo games like the one-foot-high kick and the seal walk. Soon they were warm, although their breath froze into snow mist.

Cyd came out of the house with Sisuaq in her woman's parka. She passed out snacks to the hungry children.

Kupaaq looked for the sun on November the 20th but it did not come up. In the darkness the house glowed blue and cast purple shadows. Hoarfrost clung to buildings, telephone poles, snowplows, and Kupaaq's blue hat. Icicles hung from his dad's beard. The moon did not set. The long night was upon the Arctic.

In its darkness Patak helped her mother, sisters, and aunts sew together sealskins to cover their *umiaq*, the Eskimo whaling boat.

Kupaaq watched Aalak mend the boat's wooden frame. He listened to stories of how Kupaaq–his namesake–had rescued hunters being carried out to sea on ice floes.

"It's a good thing to listen to the elders," said Kupaaq looking into the Arctic night where the wind grabbed at boys, and polar bears waited to catch them.

After two months of darkness, blizzards, and subzero cold, on January the 23rd Kupaaq and his classmates wrote, "Welcome back, Sun." The long night had ended. The children held up their hands and let the sunlight in through their fingertips. They sang an ancient Eskimo song:

Aii, Aii
There is only one great thing
The only thing
To live and see the great day that dawns
And the light that fills the world.
Aii, Aii.

Although the Arctic is different, the dawn is the same to all people. It is the light that fills the world.

"Aii, Aii," sang Kupaaq. "Aii, Aii. Welcome, Sun, welcome."

Acknowledgments

Thanks to the Harry Brower family for giving my grandson his Inupiat name and bringing him into their beautiful culture. —J. C. G.

Thanks to Craig, Cyd, Luke, and Sam for their invaluable assistance in making this book possible. —W. G. M.

ISBN 0-590-81014-6

Published by Scholastic Inc., 555 Broadway, New York, NY 10012, by arrangement with Hyperion Books for Children.
TRUMPET and associated logos are trademarks and/or registered trademarks of Scholastic Inc.

12 11 10 9 8 7 6 5 4 3 2 1 8 9/9 0 1 2 3/0

Printed in the U.S.A. 24

First Scholastic printing, October 1998

The artwork for each picture is prepared using watercolor on cold press board.
This book is set in 18-point Centaur with 65-point Bodoni Italic Swash initial caps.
Designed by Wendell Minor.

The Eskimo song on the preceding page was translated by Tegoodligak, South Baffin Island.